C000138482

50 Easy Business Hacks

To

Increase Your Sales Today

Michael Rust

Dedication

Especially for my girls Lianne, Hannah, and Aimee

And in memory of my mum and best friend Bob.

Table of Contents

Why don't **YOU** start your online business today?

We have everything you need.

The FUTURE Generation of Ebusiness in a Box

https://sc450.isrefer.com/go/p3/-bookstoread

Introduction

Sometimes the smallest of changes or tweaks can make a world of difference in your business. A business can go from not doing so well to potentially doing great with the right tweak in the right area.

That's precisely why we put together these 50 top marketing and business tips and hacks from top marketing experts in the world to hopefully inspire you to start testing out some of them to improve your business. We put them together in a way where they're super easy to read and implement by explaining the tip, giving you examples, and finally giving you a takeaway for each tip.

Don't feel like you have to implement all of the tips. Often times just putting a couple into action at a time can have drastic effects in your business. So enjoy this book and start taking action on these 50 business tips!

1. Increase Your Price Point

Most people tend to undercharge for their services. Try increasing your prices, as a test, and see what happens. Funnily enough, most people perceive something that is higher priced as being of higher quality, which can encourage people to buy your product or service. As you increase your prices, you're also receiving more per sale, increasing your profit margin. Take this strategy a step further and target higher value clients.

For example, if you run a business coaching company, and you currently charge $200 an hour for your time, increase your rates to $1000. With the perceived higher quality and value in your coaching, target businesses that make a lot of money vs. those that are barely getting by. In this example, one client would be worth 5 of your clients in the past. Not only have you raised your hourly rate but you've decreased the amount of work you need to do to earn the same amount of money.

Takeaway: Increase your prices and target customers who have more money to spend on your product/service.

2. Make Your Offer A Premium Or "Done-For-You" Offer And Charge A Premium Price

See what you can add to your offer, or bundle it with, to make it a more premium offer. Or, look at how you can make your offer more "done-for-you." Now price your offer respectively. The kicker is that more people like to buy a premium offer than a basic offer, as it's more appealing and more "done-for-you" than just an item that they'd have to do all the rest of the work on themselves. And less people offer premium services/offers, so you're competing against less.

For example, instead of charging $5 to write an article, charge $497 to $997+ to write five articles, create a blog, post the articles up, optimize it for their keywords, and have a custom graphic or two. If you were to outsource a $5 article for $3, the first example only gives you a $2 profit, or if you were to write it yourself, you'd be trading $5 for 30 minutes, at best, of your time ($10 an hour on the higher end if you're super fast). However, if you were to offer the second, more premium example, you could outsource the articles for $15, allocate $10 for some custom graphics on Fiverr.com, and put in $25 to $50 to outsource the custom blog with SEO (blogger.com blogs, for instance, can be made in a matter of minutes). That's a raw cost of $50 to $100 for a $400 to $950 profit. Or, if you were to do the work mostly yourself, you'd be talking about maybe 3 to 5 hours of work, easily putting you in the range of earning $100 to $200+ per hour compared to $10 per hour just selling a $5 article.

Takeaway: Look at how you can make your offer a premium or "done-for-you" offer by adding more things to your service or bundling your products together to give more value. This then allows you to increase your prices substantially, your premium pricing reflecting your premium product.

3. End Your Prices With A 7, .97, 5, or .95

Instead of charging $10, for instance, consider charging $9.97. Even though it's only a few cents less, people seem to think that it sounds cheaper. Even on high priced items the same tricks can work. For instance, you've probably never seen a car advertised for $30,000. Instead, you'll see it advertised for something like $29,995.

Amazingly enough, on that last example, some people will walk away thinking that the car is $29,000 in their head (even though they're smart enough to know that it's obviously $30,000).

In the past many marketers have used 9 or .99 to end the numbers in, but it seems that there's been a growing trend lately that 7, .97, 5, or .95 seem to stand out even more and appear even less expensive. Crazy stuff, but it can definitely work. And it's doubtful that you'll miss those few cents after increasing your conversions.

Takeaway: Consider adjusting your price points to end in 7, .97, 5, or .95 to make your prices seem cheaper and help increase conversions.

4. Offer Limited Time Deals

Offer limited time deals, especially ones that don't last more than a few days tops. And if you have an e-mail list, mail them a lot more on the final day with reminders to the deadline. You'll often get most of your sales on the final day! Countdown timers can be another great way to emphasize this. The idea is similar to furniture stores that seem to always have sales that end on the weekend... even though we all know they'll probably have another sale in a week or two, we're more likely to buy now if we think there's a sale on it now vs. later. People like to procrastinate, so limited time deals can get them off their butt to take action.

For example, if you run a gym, you may run a sale on gym membership, where if they sign up over the next 3 days they receive a discount on the total price, or X amount of personal training sessions as a bonus. The time limit creates a sense of urgency, encouraging people to buy that may have sat on the fence or procrastinated otherwise.

Takeaway: Create a time sensitive deal where people only have a limited time to take you up on it. The sense of urgency encourages people to buy. If you have an email list, constantly remind people of the deadline, as often the most sales will happen in the last day near the end.

5. Use The Word "Only" Before A Price

How items are described and the words we use to frame situations can have a big impact on how we then think about a scenario. Just as saying, "I cut my finger, but there's only a little blood" versus, "I cut my finger and there's blood everywhere," paint two very different pictures, the words you use to describe your pricing can make a difference to your sales. Something as small as just putting the word "only" before your pricing can increase your sales.

For example, if your price point is $97, instead write "Only $97." Psychologically, by putting "only" in front of the price, you are making little of the price, implying that it isn't that big, and is a good deal.

Takeaway: Use the word "only" before your price (e.g., "Only $97" vs. "$97") as psychologically it implies the value you are getting is greater than the small amount you are paying.

6. Mention A Savings Next To A Price Point

It is important to point out when you are giving people a discount or savings. This lets them know you're giving them a great deal and lots of value. A discount also has a psychological effect - we feel we are getting a better deal and are more likely to buy. Seeing that an item is discounted not only is an incentive to buy it now, it can also encourage new users to buy that might otherwise have not considered it.

For example, when listing your price, you might write: "$97 --- 50% Off Today!" This makes people feel they are getting a great deal, helps them justify the purchase to themselves and is more likely to push them over the line.

Takeaway: Put a savings amount next to a price point (e.g., "$97 --- 50% Off Today!) as it makes customers feel they are getting a great deal and can encourage customers to buy that may not have bought before.

7. Mention The "Normal" Price Next To Your Sales Price

When people see the difference, between your normal price and your sales price, it influences their decision to purchase. By having a "normal" price listed it creates the impression that the deal they are getting is awesome. They're getting all this value at a price that is way less than "normal". People love to believe they are getting a bargain and by listing both your normal and sale price side by side, it highlights the value they're getting for their money.

For example, when you list your pricing, write it as, "Normally $197 -- Only $97 Today!"

Takeaway: People love a bargain. Create the perception of a great deal by listing your "normal" price next to your sales price (e.g., "Normally $197 -- Only $97 Today!").

8. Offer A Range Of Differently Priced Upsells

Upselling is offering a complimentary or upgraded version of a product/service that a customer is currently purchasing. One of the most well known upsells can be heard when you head into your local fast food joint, "Would you like fries with that?" Even not so great upsells can add a quick 33% or more to your revenue stream. Some really good upsells or funnels can even double your initial sales or more! An upsell is a great way to increase the total value of a sale.

For example, if you run a dance school, and each class is $15, you could provide a number of upsells. You could offer 3 different upsells, of varying amounts:

Upsell 1 - 4 week course for $50

Upsell 2 - Gold Membership where for $120 a month you can attend as many classes as you like.

Upsell 3 - Pro dance package for $200 a month, which allows you to attend unlimited classes and receive 2 private classes a month.

Takeaway: Offer a range of differently priced upsells to customers to increase the total of each sale. Upsells are complimentary or better options on an offer a customer is already purchasing.

9. Partner With Other Businesses

Look to partner with others where both of you could make a lot of money off of each other, but whom you don't directly compete with.

For example, if you sell homemade candles, reach out to boutiques to see if they'd be willing to sell your candles (even without them buying them first - just sharing in the sales). Or if you sell a social media management or SEO service, reach out to web design firms that might not offer your services to their clients, but offer them a good chunk of the sales PLUS offer to do all the work, support, etc. for their customers AND let them market it as their own (a win-win for both). Or if you're a programmer or have a tool of your own, reach out to market leaders in your industry who might be able to sell a lot of your product and let them white label it (sell it as their own) for a good cut of the profits while you just maintain it and do support for it. One good deal here can be more than a full-time living or a good little business all by itself.

Takeaway: Look for other businesses that you don't directly compete with that you could partner with. Then look at how them selling your product can be a win-win, whether it's a share in sales, fulfilling a need their clients have but they don't offer and allowing them to market the service as their own or white labelling your product for their clients.

10. Identify What Your Competitors Are Doing Well And See How You Can Replicate It

Find out where your competitors are advertising, spy on their sales funnels, and see how you can replicate any of their good ideas that appear to be working well. There are many online tools to find out what ads and keywords your competitors are using. There's also a couple of basic ways to see what your competitors are up to - follow them on social media and subscribe to their blogs and newsletters. If they have smaller priced items, you may choose to purchase one of their items to see what their purchase process is like, whether they offer upsells, what those are and what their follow up process is to a sale. See what they are doing really well and look for how you can replicate it or adapt it to your business.

For example, if you sign up to a competitor's newsletter, you can see how they nurture a lead and turn it onto a sale. Is there anything you see in this process that is working well that you can adopt for your business?

Or you may purchase a small item from them and find they are offering a great upsell - is that something you could do?

Takeaway: Find out where and how your competitors are advertising and what their sales funnels are. Then look at what they are doing well and see how you can replicate this for your business.

11. Instead Of Waiting For Leads To Come To You, Go To Them!

Instead of just building an opt-in page or a squeeze page and waiting for leads to sign-up or reach out to you - or instead of waiting for people to find your store and buy from you - actively go out and find prospects.

Look for questions that are being asked, which are relevant to what your business provides, on forums, Q&A sites (like Yahoo Answers) and social media such as Facebook and Twitter.

Now take a couple of minutes to answer those questions, making sure you provide value first and foremost. This will help you gain extra exposure for your business, help build you up as an authority in your niche, start to build trust between you and possible customers and potentially land you some sales.

For example, if you have an SEO service, look for questions on the best ways to optimize websites. Then you could leave an answer such as, "Here are 3 tips I find work well…(insert your tips here). If you're after more information, I help people with their SEO, through information and doing it all for them, and here's a link to an article I wrote listing 17 tested ways to improve your search engine optimisation." You've already given great information and value in your answer, making people more likely to click through to your site.

Takeaway: Go looking for leads, instead of waiting for them to come to you. Look on forums, Q&A sites (like Yahoo Answers) and social media (such as Facebook, Twitter, etc) to find questions being asked that are relevant to your offer. Answer those questions, providing good value, to increase your exposure and potentially make sales.

12. Join Relevant Facebook Groups In Your Niche And See What People Are Complaining About

Find relevant Facebook groups in your niche, join them, and take the time to see what people are complaining about. What are the common complaints that keep coming up again and again? What product or service could you come up with to provide a solution to these complaints? Once you've come up with a solution, sell it or give it away for free to build a list or following.

For example, if you run a wedding planning business, join Facebook groups in that niche and see what the common complaints among brides-to-be are. Perhaps they find that it's very overwhelming, trying to remember everything to organise and knowing when to do what. You could create a timeline checklist, of what to organise when in the countdown to the big day, and offer it free to build a list of potential clients.

Takeaway: Join Facebook groups within your niche and see what the most common complaints are. Then find a solution to these complaints and either sell it or use it to build a list or following by giving it away free.

13. Use Case Studies In Your Marketing To Sell People Without Selling Them

Social proof is a great way to help sell your product. A testimonial from a satisfied customer can sometimes be more effective than you, yourself, talking about your offer. A great way to make your marketing less "salesy" while still being powerful is to include case studies from people who have used your product/services.

For example, instead of talking about how people need to buy your SEO service, write up an article, blog post, or Facebook post on how one business went from no rankings to #1 rankings and more sales in under 2 weeks with a handful of easy tweaks... and then talk about the process and what your service did. A handful of readers will naturally want to reach out to you to have you do the same thing for them.

Takeaway: Use case studies to explain your service/product and the results customers can achieve. Do this through articles, blog posts or Facebook posts.

14. Give Something Away Of Value (And Monetize The Backend)

Everybody loves a freebie! What do you currently sell, that is of value, that you could offer for free? And how can you monetize the back end of that? This works especially well if you can offer something that other businesses would normally charge for.

For example, if you have a corporate cleaning business, you could offer your first clean free, and follow up with your customer to see if they were happy with your service and would like you to continue. This is a great way to get new clients to try your service, as you're taking all the risk out of it for them and, if you do a great job, chances are they'll want to keep you on. The principle of reciprocity comes into play here too - you've given something of value to them and chances are they'll feel the urge to do the same back.

Takeaway: Find something you can give away, that has value, and then look at how you can monetize the back end.

Whether it is a sample of your service or a physical product, this works especially well if it something that other people usually charge for.

15. Bundle Your Services To Create A "Package Deal"

Look at how you can bundle your service or products together to create a package deal. This can be a great way to move more products and services and add value to your customers. Customers feel they are getting a great deal, as they are paying less than if they bought each item separately, and you get the benefit of a higher dollar sale per transaction. Bundling can also help you move slow-moving products and give you an upsell to offer to customers that may have been looking at purchasing an individual item.

For example, if you own a travel agency, offer a package deal where accommodation, flights, several meals and an attraction are all included. For another example, if you own a beauty salon, offer a pampering package, where a hair styling, manicure and massage are offered together. While a customer may have been considering purchasing one or two of these items, if you offer a great deal, they might be persuaded to purchase the whole package.

Takeaway: Bundle several of your services or products together to create a package deal. This creates another offering for your customers, with great perceived value, and gives you the opportunity to upsell, move slow-moving products and increase your dollar value per sale.

16. Approach Your Current Customers With A Complimentary Offer

It's often a lot easier to sell to your current customers than to get a new customer. They already like and trust you and know your product/service works. Tap into that opportunity by looking at what else you can sell to your customers that compliments what they bought previously.

For example, if you have a resume writing service, you could go out to recent customers and also offer an additional service where you submit their resume to X amount of job ads and write a customized cover letter for each ad, and also submit their resume to several recruitment agencies.

Takeaway: Reselling to your current customers is often a lot easier and less costly that trying to obtain a new customer. Reach out to your current and past clients with a complimentary offer to what they've bought in the past.

17. Ask For Referrals From Your Customers

Have you ever tried a product or service based on the word of a friend, colleague or family member? Many of us have, because we trust that person and are more likely to take their recommendation over someone we don't know. This is the power of referrals. Ask your current customers if they have friends, family, or people they know that they think would love your service, then contact those people on behalf of them, offering your services/products.

For example, say you have an ecommerce business where you sell natural beauty products. You could email out to your customers, asking them if they know anyone that would love your products as much as they do. If so, ask them to pass on the email address of those people and explain you'll not only offer their friend a free sample of your most popular product, but that they themself will receive a bonus 15% off their next purchase online as a thank-you. When you email the new lead with your free sample offer, mention that their friend thought they'd like your products, which is why you're emailing and would love to offer them this free sample as a gift.

Takeaway: Ask your customers if they know people they think would love your product/service, and if they'd be willing to pass their contact info on to you. Contact those people on their behalf and make them a special offer.

18. Have A Loyalty Program

A loyalty program is a great way to encourage customers to keep purchasing from you, make them feel special and reward and thank them for their continued business. Most loyalty programs involve rewarding customers when they buy regularly from you or have purchased a certain amount from you, whether it's in free products or discounted future purchases.

For example, think of your local coffee place. Many local coffee shops have a simple punch-card loyalty program, where you purchase 5 coffees and receive your 6th coffee free. The reward, of the free 6th coffee, encourages people to keep coming back to the same coffee place to indulge in their caffeine kick.

Takeaway: Implement a loyalty program that rewards customers, through free products/services or discounts for future purchases, when they regularly purchase from you.

19. Use Future-Use Coupons

When customers make a purchase, give them a coupon for a dollar value or percentage off their next purchase. This is called a "future-use" coupon. It encourages your customers to come back and purchase from you again, and keeps you in their mind. You can even make receiving the coupon dependent on spending a certain amount, to encourage customers to spend more per sale.

For example, if you have tennis shop, you could have an offer where if they spend over $100 today they get $15 off their next purchase of $100 or more. Not only does this give an incentive for your customers to spend $100 now, it also gets you an additional $100 sale next time they come in wanting to use their coupon.

Takeaway: Encourage customers to come back to you with "future-use" coupons. This is where, if they spend a certain amount with you today, they get a percentage or dollar discount next time they make a purchase with you.

20. Membership Program

A membership program is where your customers sign up, either for free or for a fee, to be part of a community or elite club. As an incentive to sign up they often receive special discounts, invites to product launches, early access and other rewards. The benefit to you is that by offering incentives and rewarding customers' loyalty, you encourage them to keep coming back to you and buying from your business. You also have the benefit of beginning to build a list of clients that you can regularly market to and offer deals to.

For example, if you have an online store and sell health food products, you could create a VIP membership program for customers, where one of the main benefits is free shipping. You could also offer special deals, such as a free gift (perhaps a sample of a new product you want to promote) with each purchase over $30. The free shipping encourages people to join your VIP Membership Program, now allowing you to continue to regularly market to them, and the free gift with purchase offer incentivizes them to purchase from you.

Takeaway: Create a membership program, where your customers become part of a community, and receive special benefits, (e.g., free shipping, early access to sales, special deals, free gifts with purchase). This allows you to start to build a list of leads and customers to market to and also encourages customers to continue to purchase from you.

21. Offer A Free Gift With Purchase

Offering a free gift, with a purchase over a certain amount, is a great way to encourage people to buy from you, but also to spend more per sale. A great way to take this strategy a step further is to make your free gift a sample of other products you want to promote, or a new product you want to encourage your customers to try so as to buy in the future.

For example, beauty brands use this strategy regularly, and to great effect, offering a selection of sample size beauty products in a cute looking case, when spending over $50, $70, $100, etc., in one transaction. Not only does the free gift encourage their customers to buy more beauty products in one transaction, it also allows them a chance to introduce their customers to new products or items they may not have bought previously, without the chance to try them first.

Takeaway: Look at what you can offer as a free gift to customers when they spend over a certain dollar amount in one transaction. This encourages your customer to spend more per sale and also gives you a chance to get customers trying new products, if you make those products your gift.

22. Offer A Guarantee

Offering a guarantee is a great way to make it easier for customers to buy. It takes the risk out of the purchase for them, as it gives them an out if they don't like the product. Psychologically, it also gives them confidence in your product - as why would you be offering a guarantee if you weren't confident in your product? Now, to be clear, make sure you do offer a great product before you whack an awesome guarantee on it!

For example, if you have a mattress company, you could offer a guarantee and word it like this: "Try our mattresses risk free for 30 days - In the unlikely event that you're not 100% satisfied with your mattress we will give you 100% of your money back." A guarantee like this takes the risk out of buying for your customers and gives them confidence in your product. Most people won't take advantage of the guarantee and the amount of returns you'll have versus the increase in sales will be well worth it.

Takeaway: Offer a guarantee that takes the risk out of the purchase for the customer (make sure you have a good quality product that you're willing to back). Make your guarantee bold and visible, and the amount of extra sales should far outweigh those that make use of the guarantee.

23. Focus On The Benefits Of Your Product/Service

In your marketing, focus on the benefits of your service, instead of the features. It's the benefits that sell your product, not the features. For example, does a person buying an anti-aging cream want to know that it contains the ingredient Q10 or that it visibly reduces wrinkles and makes them look younger? Think about how you can use the benefits your product provides in your marketing - you can still list the features, but link them to the benefit that the feature will give your customer.

For example, if you have a business selling a course teaching guitar lessons, you might have 3 main features that you could translate into benefits for your students:

Feature 1: Over 50 pages of guitar lessons

Benefit 1: Learn to play the guitar in under 3 hours!

Feature 2: Get training on how songs are made

Benefit 2: You'll be able to create your very own songs!

Feature 3: Practice on over a dozen songs with step by step instructions

Benefit 3: You'll be able to play over a dozen top songs in no time!

Each time, you emphasis what the student is actually getting out of the feature by explaining the end result that they'll receive from the feature.

Takeaway: In your marketing, look at how you can emphasize the benefits that customers receive from your service, as opposed to focusing on the features. You can still list the features, as they are important, especially with certain products, but link them to what the customers will get out of that feature. Why should the customer care about that feature - what end result does it deliver to them?

24. Ask For Feedback From Your Customers

Ask for feedback from your customers and see what the common themes are. What do your customers like most about your product? How can you focus on that more in your marketing? What do they believe that your product/service currently lacks? Think about how you can use their feedback to create a new/improved service and offer that to your customers.

For example, perhaps you have a business that creates websites and the common feedback that your customers give is that they wish you also helped rank their site on search engines. You could create an additional service, where for a monthly fee you help rank their website. If you don't know how to do this yourself, you could always outsource this part, but white label it as your own service - you still make a profit on the service, but don't need to do any of the work. You can offer this to your current customers, saying that due to their feedback and the demand, you've created this service to help them with what they want most.

Takeaway: Ask for feedback from your customers, specifically on what they like most and what they dislike most/wish you offered. Use the feedback on what they like most, and highlight it in your marketing. With what they like least/wish you did, create an additional or improved service/product and offer it to your customers.

25. Offer Free Trials/Demonstration Of Products

Sometimes it's hard to see the benefit of something we haven't seen in action or tried first. Offering a free trial period, or a demonstration of your product, can be a great way to alleviate a potential customer's fears and make them confident the product will work for them. Also, once someone has tried something free they often feel obliged to reciprocate by purchasing from you - it's the principle of reciprocity in action.

For example, if you have a software company, offer a free 30 day trial, so customers can see how it works, use it and see the results they get from it. You'll get customers who may have sat on the fence or not purchased previously, ready to buy because they can get a chance to experience how great the product can actually be for them.

Takeaway: Make it easy for customers to see the value in your product and purchase from you by offering a free trial or demonstration of your product. You'll get a chance to make them feel comfortable with your product and see how great it is for them, before having to lay down their hard earned cash. This in turn leads to more sales, especially from people who may have been skeptical about your product without the chance to try it first.

26. Reduce/Offer Free Shipping Within A Certain Time Frame

Don't you hate it when you're searching for an item, find it at an amazing price, then see that shipping is going to cost you an arm and a leg? One way to increase your sales, especially over a short period of time, is to reduce the cost of your shipping, or offer a sale period time where shipping is free. By putting a time limit on when you make free shipping available, you add a sense of urgency, encouraging customers to buy now, as opposed to at a later date. It's also a good way to encourage customers who may have been on the fence to make a purchase now.

For example, say you have a business that sells gardening supplies online. Reach out to your customers and let them know that for any supplies ordered by midnight on Sunday, you'll offer free delivery. If you have regular customers that place large orders with you, you may even want to reach out and call them. On your website, make sure it's clear that you have this offer available for a limited time - it may be a pop up on your website or the first thing your customer sees.

Takeaway: For a limited time offer reduced or free shipping on products. The limited time frame creates a sense of urgency, encouraging customers to purchase now, as opposed to at a later date, and encourages customers who may have been on the fence to make the purchase.

27. Offer A Themed Promotion (Seasonal, Holiday, Etc.)

Any special promotions can help you drive sales, especially those sitting on the fence as to whether or not to buy from you. However, offering seasonal or holiday themed promotions can help even more, as prospects not only immediately understand that it's a limited time deal for a good reason, but you'll also hit them up during a peak buying period.

For example, the vast majority of people are probably already buying lots of stuff over Christmas, Valentine's Day, Black Friday, etc., so you can ride that wave while they already have their credit cards out, while also standing out amongst the crowd of competitors by having something that they perceive as a special deal.

Similar to other promotions, it's often best to have these be very limited time deals (even if you bring them back multiple times) so prospects don't have the opportunity to sit on the fence too long. Three or so days is often the perfect amount of time to offer a special promotional deal, as long as you give them many reminders along the way. For instance, if you have an email list and are offering a three day special promotional offer, we recommend mailing once on day 1, twice on day 2, and three times on day 3. Using this method will get you a lot of sales on that last day, especially during the last hours when they know there's no time left!

Takeaway: During holidays, different seasons, or any other special time of the year, it's a good idea to create themed promotions with special offers to not only drive extra sales, but to also stand out from the rest of the competition during high sales periods.

28. Send A "We Haven't Seen You In A While" With A Thank You And An Incentive

Most businesses tend to practically ignore their prospects and even their best clients. This is a horrible thing to do, as you'd be leaving a ton of money on the table in doing so.

One thing that you can do to help remind your prospects and customers about you is to send either an e-mail or a card with something like a thank you note along with an incentive to take some further action (like a discount or a freebie leading into a sales offer of yours).

For instance, if you have leads that haven't bought from you but who've expressed an interest of some kind, you can either automatically (via an autoresponder) or manually follow-up with them by writing an e-mail saying how you haven't seen them in a while, want to thank them for previously reaching out, and then letting them know about either a freebie you're currently offering, which can lead into a paid offer, or a discount or other incentive/deal that you currently have. This can help revive old, "dead" leads into being active buyers.

Likewise, if you have existing clients that bought one of your offerings but haven't been active since, you can send them a thank you for being a customer along with a similar freebie or special discount/offer exclusively for your members/customers into some other offer you have. This can be a great and easy way to make more sales without a ton of effort.

Takeaway: Follow up with old leads and past customers with a "we haven't seen you in a while" message, thank you note, etc., along with a freebie, incentive, or discount to help drive more sales from them your way while also making them feel appreciated at the same time.

29. Start An Affiliate Program

Want a way to make sales without paying for any ads and with zero risk of losing money in doing so? The obvious answer is a big YES, but very few business owners take advantage of running their own affiliate programs, which can do exactly that!

Affiliate programs are where you offer others a cut of any sale that they send your way. When this is done online, there's traditionally special "affiliate links" that they get from you. When they send people through those links that later buy from your site, they'd get credited for and paid a percentage of the sale. You can do a similar concept offline just by letting others refer your prospects directly (and manually crediting them), or even by handing out special "unique" coupon codes to others to hand out to their prospects so you know where they came from. This could be a special coupon that you hand out, with a code or ID on it, so you know where it came from. Regardless, in either case you only pay them after a sale is made, which makes it virtually risk free for you.

With the online route, there's various places you can sign up to that will put your offer on their network, like Clickbank.com, Amazon.com (which is great to sell on just by itself), CJ.com, etc., as they can instantly let affiliates sign-up for and start promoting your offers. Alternatively, there's also private affiliate programs/scripts out there that you can get free or for fairly cheap to run your own affiliate program without the need for another network.

Regardless of which route you go, don't expect to magically get lots of affiliates signing up and promoting your offer without you raising a finger. It can take some work to reach out and recruit these affiliates to get them promoting you. It's best to reach out to those who you can also help in return first, as well as to make sure that you truly have a great converting offer with good payouts to make your offer attractive to these affiliates.

Takeaway: Create an affiliate program and recruit affiliates to help promote your offers at little to no risk to you. Ensure you have attractive offers and payouts, and that you proactively reach out to the best affiliate prospects out there.

30. Offer Free Review Copies to Influencers Like Bloggers, Big Pinterest Users, Etc.

Did you know that some big influencers out there online can literally drive millions of dollars in sales, with a single post on social media, or mention on a big blog? In fact, there's even billion-dollar businesses that have gotten their start from single big influencers mentioning their products.

And, surprisingly enough, it's easier to do than you might think. Sure, it might be far harder to do a multi-million dollar launch overnight from a big star mentioning you just to be nice, but there's plenty of well-known influencers that can still drive a ton of sales your way (and you never know when you might get lucky by landing a bigger one).

To increase your chances of this, you should take the time to reach out to these big influencers, blogs, news sites, etc., and offer them your products for free in the hopes that they'd be willing to review them.

Sometimes you can even pay these influencers to mention your products. And although some of the biggest influencers out there cost some serious money to do that, others will do it for virtually pennies on the dollar (think about it - $100 or so for a minute or two of their time is a very good deal for some even semi well known influencers).

Not sure how to find these influencers? Don't over think it! Search social media sites like Facebook, Twitter, Pinterest, YouTube, etc., on top of forums, blogs, big news sites, magazines, etc., and then reach out to them directly on those sites (either via messaging or finding an e-mail address).

Takeaway: Take the time to identify and reach out to influencers and big sites to see if they'd be willing to mention your product (even if for a price) or review it for a free copy. Just a couple of deals can create a big boost in sales for you!

31. Go For The Big Fish Deals

Too often business owners try to fight over the scraps. They try to make deals or land sales with anyone and everyone that they can find, regardless of if those deals are barely worth any money to them.

It's amazing what can happen when you try to go for the bigger clients or choose bigger businesses to partner with. Just a single deal can often make for a very good month (or even year!).

There's two main ways of doing this. First, you can target more high-end prospects with higher end offerings. Similar to some prior tips we gave about raising your prices and offering more "done for you" services and products, you can try to target the elite buyers instead of focusing on being the low-priced leader barely scraping by. The second way is to try to focus on big "competitors," or on other business owners who are far bigger than you in a similar market, but not necessarily competing, and then trying to strike a deal with them to sell or promote your offers (for a big cut). If you make this hands-free, super easy, and very profitable for them, you'd be surprised how many are willing to do deals with you.

One way of doing the second suggestion here is by offering to white label your product or service. This is where you allow someone to sell your offer as their own while you do all the work to fulfill it. This can be a win-win for both, as they can get a good cut of the sale for doing virtually nothing except making easy sales for you, while you fulfill the sales, do the support, and make lots of extra sales without having to spend money on advertising or do any marketing yourself. A single big fish deal like this can make an entire business.

Takeaway: Try going for the big fish now and then, whether by going after more elite prospects, at higher prices with better offers, or by seeking out big partnerships to do white label deals, where they sell your offers for you for a cut.

32. Ask Your Prospects And Clients Questions On What They Want/Need

Business owners often do more talking than listening. When it comes to making sales, often it's best to do more listening than talking. Instead of overthinking and brainstorming what your prospects might want, why not just ask them? You'd probably be surprised at how easy it can be to sell them what they're already telling you they most want/need.

For example, if you're selling a variety of online marketing or web services, instead of trying to force them to buy a particular SEO package to help rank their site, why not ask them what they think their biggest issues are right now with their business? You might find that they really don't care much about their ranking but might instead be focused on their social media, e-mail list management, or some other service that you could easily do for them.

Once someone tells you what their issues are, ask them what they think that would do for their business if those issues were solved, and then ask them how much more they think they could make with all of those things being fixed and running smoothly. This lets THEM tell YOU the value those services mean to them rather than you trying to convince them of the value that you can bring to the table. The more you talk about yourself or your services instead of just listening to what their needs are, the less likely you are to typically land those sales.

And, as an added bonus, this method works well both for prospects who've never bought from you, as well as for existing customers that you could sell other things to. For instance, you might find that all of your clients of one service are practically begging to buy a different service if only you offered it! And this might be incredibly easy for you to either offer or outsource.

Takeaway: Ask your prospects and clients what their needs are and what would help them the most and then provide them with a product/service that fulfills that need. Do more listening than talking to land the most sales.

33. Look To Outsource Other Offers/Services That You Can Sell Yourself

There's only so much time in the day, and although it can be a great idea to add extra services that you sell and fulfill yourself, it's not always practical. This is why it can be a great idea to look for other services or offers that you can sell yourself but easily outsource to others to do with little to no work on your part.

For instance, you might be a web designer that often gets requests to create and add videos to your clients' sites, but it might either be very time consuming or nearly impossible for you to create nice looking videos to sell as a service even if you could get hundreds to thousands of dollars per sale for them.

Instead of just passing on that easy money, why not look for others online who already offer those services, reach out to them, markup their prices (or make them more "done for you" to increase the value and prices you can charge) and get permission to use their testimonials, social proof, examples, sales pages, etc. as your own (or that you can modify) to sell to your own clients. This can be a great way of making extra money at huge margins.

For instance, there's often places online like Fiverr.com, Craigslist.com, Freelancer.com, etc., that have tons of workers for almost anything you can think of. In some cases, you can find workers who can make nice looking videos, for $25 to $50 (less in some cases) and you could turn around and sell that service for hundreds to even thousands of dollars.

Adding a couple of these services of your own can be super easy, add almost no work to your plate, but make you a fortune almost completely hands free!

Takeaway: Be on the lookout for other services or offers that you can sell that you're able to outsource to others for pennies on the dollar. This can add some easy money to your sales funnels without adding extra work for you to do.

34. Offer Premium Support Services (White Glove, Warranties, Free Upgrades, Etc.)

You've probably bought electronics before and been offered the purchase an additional warranty. Or maybe you've purchased furniture before and been offered a white glove service to deliver and setup your new couch.

These are all examples of premium support services that can have very large profit margins, so even if only a smaller percentage of customers take you up on them, they can add a lot to your bottom line.

Some of these premium support services can be at little to no cost to you. For instance, one business we've seen had a warranty offer where you could get free replacement charger cables forever on your phone, if they ever fail, for a small one time extra fee as long as you just cover the small shipping and handling fee. However, these cables have such huge margins anyway that the small S&H fee literally covered the cost of the cables and the shipping.Tthe "warranty" that was sold was essentially 100% pure profit, despite how it would appear to be an awesome deal for the buyers (paying $5 for S&H instead of $29 for a new cable sounds like, and is, a pretty good deal).

Another example would be offering faster support, faster shipping, faster service, etc. All of these can have huge margins for little to no extra work!

Takeaway: Try to brainstorm at least a couple of extra premium support services that you can offer your buyers (like extra warranties, faster support, faster service, etc.) that come with huge margins despite not really increasing your costs much, if at all.

35. Offer Free Plus Shipping & Handling Products

One of the best things you can do to get people to take action, especially online, is to offer a free plus shipping & handling offer. These offers have an obvious HUGE value because nothing beats free, and by having them pay a small S&H fee, they still see the value in the free product, despite how often times your products' costs might be completely covered in this S&H fee.

For instance, if you go to a site like Aliexpress.com, which specializes in drop-shipping products of all sorts, you can find lots of jewelry, pet toys, gadgets, etc. for under $2 that already include free shipping. Some of these have perceived values of easily $10 to $30 or more.

That means that your customers get an awesome deal by thinking they got the bargain of a lifetime, while you also get a steal of a deal by getting a new customer at better than no cost to you (if the product and shipping costs $2, for instance, you're up $3 in profit just by charging a $5 S&H fee).

Obviously, it's hard to strike it rich at a few bucks at a time, which is why you want to treat these offers as only an entry point into your sales funnel/offers. You want to offer them additional upsells, other products/services on your backend, and take full advantage of their e-mail address to reach out with additional offers in the future, as everything from that point on could be pure profit for you (at least in terms of no advertising costs).

Takeaway: Consider an impulse buy product with a free plus S&H offer where you don't lose money after collecting the small S&H charge. Then upsell them additional offers to make the most of your money.

36. Consider Adding Physical Products As A Bonus, Especially For Your Digital Offers Or Services

Selling digital products like e-books or videos (or even services) can be great, as they often carry much higher margins than physical products. However, people often place a much higher value on physical products that they can touch and hold.

This doesn't mean that you have to offer all your products as physical ones -- far from it! Instead, you should consider offering a simple physical product like a branded coffee mug, hat, t-shirt, or some other product that makes sense with your offer, as a bonus for those who take action fast.

This does two things. First, it makes people take action faster because they know there's probably a limited quantity of the physical product (vs. a digital one that they realistically know you can have as many as you want). And second, they place a high value on physical products that they can touch.

In fact, as crazy as it sounds, you can increase conversions on a $2,000 web service simply by offering a branded coffee mug or t-shirt as a bonus. Likewise, you can even increase conversions MUCH more on lower priced offerings where you give something away that they perceive to be worth as much or more than what they're buying. For example, you could sell a newsletter for $19/month and give a free t-shirt away with any new subscriber, and that could in some cases more than double your conversions because they think the value of the shirt is worth more than the $19 they paid (and they'll often stay for a much longer time, making you a lot more money).

Another example would be if you sold a phone case for $29 and included a free charging cable with that. Since many of those sell for $29 or so themselves, the perceived value of the offer is huge, even though it might only add a dollar or two to your costs (and still give you huge margins).

You can do the same idea for services that you offer. For instance, you could offer a free cell phone clip-on lens with any purchase of a custom web video (justifying it in a way where they could shoot professional looking videos themselves from their phone).

For an offline physical product or service example, you could offer a free towel and sweatband just for trying out a one month gym membership as a trial.

You'd be shocked at how your conversions can jump even for higher priced offerings, and probably more shocked at how much they can help your lower priced offerings.

Takeaway: Consider adding physical products as bonuses to your offers, as they can tremendously increase conversions for both low and high-priced products and services.

37. Offer Different Packages/Buying Options To Increase The Perceived Value And Sales (Even With No Intention Of Selling The Others)

In many cases it can be a wise idea to offer multiple similar packages when selling something. However, instead of offering drastically different offerings, which might make your prospects hesitate more due to not being sure which option to get, you can offer similar options where the "value buy" seems like an amazing deal.

For example, let's say that you're selling an SEO service to help websites rank better. If your main offer is a done for you package for $997 where you fix up their site and offer some basic consultations for them too, that can normally seem like a lot of money to some people and can make them hesitate more on if they should buy or not. However, you could offer three options where the "basic" package is for $897 and only includes a report where you identify the issues but don't fix it for them, the "most popular" package is for $997 and includes identifying and fixing all the issues on top of three free consultation calls, and the "elite" package is for $1,997 and includes everything in the most popular package but also includes unlimited consultation calls for a month.

What this does is that almost everyone thinks that the middle, "most popular" package is the best deal. It's only a little more than the basic package, but it includes a TON of extra value. Whereas the "elite" package is twice the price but only has some extra consultation calls that most people think they'll never use. All of a sudden people perceive the $997 option as being cheap and a great deal! The other options aren't meant to necessarily get sales. They're simply meant to help make your main offer stand out more.

And by literally writing something like Basic Package, Most Popular, and Elite Package next to the options, you can help them differentiate between them even more and gravitate towards the Most Popular one.

Takeaway: Offer multiple packages like a Basic, Most Popular, and Elite Package where the value of the Most Popular one seems huge in order to make more people gravitate towards it and see it as a crazy good deal.

38. Always Be Split Testing

Too many business owners and marketers will only create one version of an offer, sales page, opt-in page, ad, etc., and simply hope that it works. If it does, they're happy. If it doesn't, they think that the offer simply doesn't work.

That's a horrible way to go about it. If your first attempt doesn't work, you'll want to create several different versions of all of those to see if maybe it's something in your sales copy. And even if you get lucky and get a winning offer right off the bat, you'll want to be constantly test new things in the sales copy to see if you can increase clicks to your ads, lead conversions to your opt-in pages, sales to your sales page, and upsells to your upsell pages.

It doesn't have to be hard. Even just changing around headlines or little things here and there can often have drastic effects. For instance, you might find that changing a headline and shortening down the length of an opt-in page might boost your lead conversions from 20% to 30%. That alone could increase your sales by 50%! And by tweaking an upsell page just a bit, you might find that you move conversions there from 5% to 8%, which would be a 60% increase on the backend! Little changes can go a long way and can easily turn a loser campaign into a winner.

Takeaway: Always be testing new sales copy and such in order to see if you can increase your opt-in rate, sales conversions, or upsell conversions. Little changes can often have drastic effects that can turn a bad campaign into a winner.

39. Run Contests

Contests can be a great way to grab more leads or prospects, get feedback or testimonials from existing customers, encourage participation or attendance on webinars, and more. And, it's not like you have to give away a car or something crazy expensive. In fact, often times cheaper giveaways will help increase your conversions even more (perhaps because they think they'll have a better chance of winning?).

For instance, you can run an ad where you're advertising a contest for a free drone that you're selling. Anyone who enters you know is probably a potential prospect, as they're interested in the drone that you sell. When you do that, you can immediately advertise a special deal you have on them in case they don't win (and offer to refund if they do) and want to get it right away. The benefit here is that you can get dirt cheap clicks and leads when advertising this way (on places like Facebook), all while building up a very targeted list.

You can also use contests as a way to build up your testimonials. Offer to enter customers into a contest when they submit any testimonials or feedback about your product. People love contests, which is why it can be a great way to get them to take action.

Takeaway: Use contests to get lots of cheap traffic and leads to check out your offers. Or, alternatively, use contests to encourage testimonials or feedback on your products.

40. Find Prospects In Forums, Q&A Sites, Blogs, and Social Media That You Can Help

Instead of waiting for prospects to find you, why not go out there and find them? One of the best ways of doing this is by searching for them in forums, Q&A sites like Yahoo Answers and Quora, social media like Facebook and Twitter, and on blogs, to name a few.

You can find prospects asking questions relevant to your niche, and asking for advice on what to purchase. By taking only a few minutes to reply on those sites, you not only help that one potential prospect out, but you ensure that dozens, hundreds, or potentially even thousands of people or more, will eventually see your response (many of whom might have the same question your original prospect did) and follow your advice to check out your site, video, or offer. The key is to provide value first and foremost, though, instead of just spamming your link or offer around.

For instance, if you're selling diamonds or are just an affiliate of a diamond site, you can seek out prospects asking questions on what to look for, if a particular diamond is a good deal or not, what sites are best, etc. When you help them, you can also drive them back to your sites or videos where you might have more information on the very questions they have, along with your links or affiliate links to your recommended diamond sites or offers. Or you could even offer to do a free service where you help pick out a few diamonds for them based on their criteria, all while having the links to your recommended ones be your affiliate links (often best to simply ask if they want your help first and then send the links over e-mail in a case like this).

And the cool part here is that you can do this on high traffic sites, sites already ranking on Google and other search engines, to ensure that your efforts have the maximum payoff by giving it the most potential to be seen by others.

Takeaway: Take the time to find places where your prospects are hanging out online and help answer their questions by leading them back to your sites, videos, or offerings.

41. Create A Spiderweb of Content And Videos Across The Web Asking And Answering All The Common Questions Your Prospects Might Have

Potential prospects of yours are often already out there online searching for the answers to their questions. For instance, if they're in the market for a moped/scooter, they're probably searching Google right now on tons of questions like what the difference is between a 50cc engine and a 150cc engine. Or what a good scooter for carrying two people is. Or what is a good all-electric moped. There are literally dozens to even hundreds of common questions that they're probably searching for answers on.

And although the prior tip talked about finding people out there already asking questions on sites like forums, many people never take the time to post up their questions and just do the research themselves. That's why it's important to make sure that you have lots of content in the form of blog posts, webpages, videos, articles, etc., where you're specifically trying to target their questions in the title of your post/video and then clearly answering the question within the body of your post or video.

If you take even a half hour a week to create some extra content and target a different keyword or question each time, you'll find that you'll often start ranking for these various question keywords and start driving lots of traffic your way to your site or offer (just make sure to recommend specific offers to them via your link or affiliate links at the end). You'll literally be creating a spiderweb of content to catch these prospects and drag them to you!

Takeaway: Create lots of content and/or videos targeting questions that your prospects are probably asking online now, and then clearly answer those questions within that content all the while recommending specific products/offers to them.

42. Take Advantage Of E-mail Marketing (More Than You Are Now)

E-mail marketing is cheap and very effective, yet few businesses truly take advantage of that. With e-mail costs literally being fractions of a percentage point of the cost of mailing flyers, postcards, etc., you'd think that businesses would be all over it. However, many only rarely, at best, use it.

Even many online marketers, who often focus on building up e-mail lists to promote their offers, don't mail their e-mail lists as often as they should. Let's face it - there's TONS of competition online. Competitors are already e-mailing your leads whether you like it or not (after all, how many lists are you on?). If you mail your lists only a couple of times a month, they'll likely forget who you are. And even if they don't, you're missing out on lots of opportunities to be mailing them on your own offers, additional offers you could market to them, affiliate offers, etc. Consider mailing at least a few times a week, if not daily (or more in some cases), especially if you could be marketing more than a single product to them.

And, above all else, make absolutely sure that you're collecting those leads, building a list, and taking full advantage of e-mail autoresponders out there. If not, you're simply being a fool and leaving a ton of money on the table.

Takeaway: Not only should you be building an e-mail list, you should be mailing them a lot more. Consider mailing at least a few times a week if not daily with several different offers mixed in.

43. Target Multiple Keywords On Multiple Different Pages Of Your Website

Most businesses do a horrible job at targeting keywords on their websites. At best they'll try to rank for a single keyword, but often times even then they don't do a good job of targeting it.

The key to ranking well and getting lots of organic traffic is to pick several keywords (a dozen or more can be a good start) where each of your pages within your website (or each of your blog posts within your blog) are trying to be optimized for a different keyword.

The best way to do this is to have the keyword you're trying to rank for on a particular page or blog post be in your title and your title tags (title tags are what show up typically in Google as the blue links in the search results - you want those to be keyword rich and appealing). If you're trying to target a term like "puppy potty training," you can add that in your title while also making it more interesting and appealing like "Puppy Potty Training - 5 Minute Trick to Potty Train Your Puppy." This lets you not only target your main keyword well on that page, but it also looks far more appealing and will be far more likely to get clicks checking out your page, which can in return help boost your rankings even more!

You could then target other puppy training type terms on other pages of your site while optimizing each and every single one of those. Similarly, if you're a lawyer and you're trying to rank your business, consider creating separate webpages within your website where each one is focused on a particular type of law that you practice while targeting keywords related to that one. For instance, one page could be targeting "Immigration Lawyer in Atlanta, GA," while another page could be targeting "Real Estate Attorney in Atlanta, GA" and so on.

On top of having good keywords and titles/title tags, you should also look into optimizing other aspects of your website like the description tags (the text below the blue links that appear in the search results of Google), schemas (more information you give Google and other search engines to rank you better and show more information like your phone number, hours, prices, etc.) and sitemaps (a table of contents for your website). If you're clueless on what all these terms are, no worries! You can always get a tool like WebFire.com that can help optimize and fix all of these issues for you (on top of other tools they have to help find you leads, create and distribute content, analyze keywords, etc.).

Takeaway: Choose a variety of keywords related to your site and target specific ones on specific pages within your site to give you the best chance of ranking for each one.

44. Use Your Consumers' Language

Business owners often get caught up in their own lingo. More often than not, they forget that their consumers probably don't understand a lot of the technical terms that they use.

The key is to try to dumb down your sales copy, advertising materials, and general sales conversations to use the everyday language of the people you're trying to most attract. For instance, even though a lot of people know that SEO stands for search engine optimization and is a way to help your websites rank better, an equal if not far larger group of people who might be looking for your SEO services don't know what any of that means! Instead of searching for "SEO services" or "SEO tools," they're probably using terms more like "rank on Google tools" or "get better rankings" or "how to show up on the first page of Google" instead. They might even just be searching for something like "how to get more sales online" or "how to get more traffic to my website."

Not only should you consider using your consumers' language in terms of what you're trying to rank for, but you should also try dumbing down your sales pitch/message as well to make sure that you're using the everyday language of the consumers whom you're trying to target. Not only will they be far more likely to come across you, but they'll often be far more likely to buy from you.

Takeaway: Try dumbing down your sales messages. Try using the everyday language of your target market instead of all the technical terms that you might currently use.

45. Be Big And Bold In Your Ads And Sales Copy

Being mediocre or boring rarely gets you anywhere in business. People are bombarded with ads and other offers all the time. You need to stand out! One way of doing that is to make sure that you're being big and bold in your advertising messages.

For instance, if you're selling a course on how to learn piano easily online, don't have an ad or headline that says something like, "Learn how to play the piano easily." That's a boring statement that will simply get overlooked next to all of the competition. Instead, consider a phrase more like, "Learn how to play the piano like a pro in 7 days or less!"

Or instead of selling a weight loss course with a headline like, "Five ways to lose weight," consider something more like, "Five breakthrough, easy weight loss techniques to lose 10 pounds in a week with minimal effort." Obviously, you want the statements to be true, but if you don't spice up your advertising and sales copy by making big, bold statements, you won't grab the attention of your prospects.

Takeaway: Go for big and bold statements in your advertising that focus on the results or benefits in an exciting way to make you stand out from the crowd. Instead of an ad that says, "Learn to play the piano easily," go for something more bold like, "Learn how to play the piano like a pro in 7 days or less!"

46. Know Your Numbers And Data

Do you know what the lifetime value of your customers are? Do you know what your costs to acquire your customers are? Do you know their average retention rate? What about your conversion rate to leads and then to sales? Do you know how much your upsells and/or backend are worth for each front-end sale? What about what your average lead is worth to you and your costs to acquire just a lead?

If you don't know the answer to ALL of those, you're likely losing a lot of money by not truly knowing your numbers. If you don't know where the areas that you can truly improve on are, you're shooting blindly hoping to get lucky and hit your target.

Often times the difference between a great campaign and a bad one is just in knowing your numbers and the true value of your customers. Imagine if you were spending $10 to acquire a $5 customer from day one. What would you do? Most would abandon that campaign and consider it a failure. But what if you knew your numbers and knew that on average, you make an additional $15 per customer on the backend within the first three months? You would effectively be tossing out a campaign that would've doubled your money.

Or, imagine if you just saw the end results and saw that you were making $12 per $10 spent, so you decide to just ramp up your ads to get richer $2 at a time, without realizing that you have awesome front-end conversions but horrible upsell conversions (or horrible opt-in rates but great sales conversions). By fixing the area that's wrong, you might be able to turn that $12 into $25 and get richer much faster.

By being able to know where your problem areas are, you can fix them much faster. If you truly know your numbers and data, creating and growing a business becomes much easier.

Takeaway: Know your numbers and data to know things like your conversion rates, lifetime values, etc., so that you can get a bigger picture of your business and what you need in order to grow faster and more profitably.

47. The Number A Customer Sees First Can Change The Entire Likelihood Of Whether They'll Buy Or Not

People's mindsets can be easily changed in several ways. One of those ways is when it comes to how they perceive the price of a product.

For example, if someone is buying a car and has a budget of $15,000, if they see a car that they like for $30,000, they're unlikely to buy it because it's over their budget by so much. Even if they first see a car for $20,000, they'd normally be unlikely to budge with their price.

However, if they see that there's a $30,000 car marked down to $20,000 through a special promotional deal, they'll be far more likely to spend more than their $15,000 budget because they think they're getting such a great deal for only a chunk more (they're saving $10,000 for spending $5,000 more).

Or let's say that you're planning on adding a stone retaining wall to your house, and in your mind you have a budget of $7,000. If a contractor comes out and says that they can do it for $10,000, you'll be likely to pass or at least wait until you get another quote. However, the contractor instead could say that normally a wall like what you want would run more like $18,000 to $20,000 depending on the stone used, but if you're willing to use a particular type of stone on sale this week and able to start next week when the contractor has a free week by chance, he could do it for $10,000. That would make the customer think that he's getting a crazy good deal because it's nearly $8,000 to $10,000 less than normal, and he's not really losing much by using a particular type of stone (which the contractor could make sure was like the style/look they want anyway) or by agreeing to do it next week instead of this week. Even if it's a few grand more than their budget, they walk away wanting to quickly take action because they think it's such a great deal.

Takeaway: The first number a customer sees can determine what type of deal they think they're getting, so make sure to have a compromise or deal where it normally is way more than their budget, but for only a bit more, they can get a huge savings in comparison to how much more they'd pay. For instance, if the budget is $5,000, don't show a $7,000 product first. Show a $12,000 product first that is on sale for $7,000 for a limited time.

48. People Act Like How You Label Them, So Label Them How You Want Them To Act

People often act how you label them. If you praise a senior for appearing strong, they'll be far more likely to perform better on a strength test. Likewise, if you act like the senior isn't strong, they'll be far more likely to perform worse on a strength test. This is despite how technically they're the exact same strength in either case! But by labeling them one way, they'll perform to those expectations (and believe it themselves).

When applying this to your marketing, try to label your prospects in a way where it gives them hope that your solution would be perfect for them. For instance, if you sell a course on how to improve your tennis game, instead of acting like they suck now and you could help them, say that just by knowing that they're looking to improve their game, you know that their mental aspect of the game is already ahead of 95% of other players, and that all they need now is to fine tune that part as well as to learn a few simple shot techniques to accelerate their game even more and be the best they can be. In this case you're making them believe that they're already ahead of others and have great potential, so they might as well take advantage of that and go even further.

Another example would be if you sell a course on investing. Instead of acting like you're a genius and everyone else is an idiot, say that just by being there and knowing a few basics that you're about to cover, they'll be smarter than 99% of others out there when it comes to investing. And then later reinforce that they're all ahead of the game and can take it to the next level by grabbing your course.

Takeaway: How you label your prospects can directly influence the actions they take and their performance. Try using that to your advantage by making them feel smart by checking your offer out, or letting them know how great they are with where they are now but how a few easy changes can make them even greater.

49. Try Selling Higher Priced Offers On Webinars

If you haven't heard of webinars, it's basically where you go on a (usually live) "video call" where you can see the presenter's screen (and sometimes them) and hear their voice. In the world of marketing, they're often used as a way to give out some content and then transitioning to try to get you to buy an offer.

Typically, prospects will go to a registration page where they enter at least their e-mail address, and then they'll later go on the live call. Usually only a portion of the traffic will register (if you can get half, that's pretty good), and even less will show up in person (if you can get a third that register to show up, that's pretty good). However, of those that do show up, they're far more likely to buy from you after watching your presentation.

It's best to use webinars to sell higher priced offers that normally aren't impulse buys. Prices from $500 to thousands of dollars tend to do really well on webinars, as the conversions tend to be a lot higher compared to a sales page or even a video sales page. If you have a sales page that isn't doing too hot, consider trying out a webinar. Or, if you have a low-priced offer, which isn't doing too well, consider raising the price and value of the offer and trying to sell it on a webinar. You'll probably be shocked at the results.

Takeaway: Especially for higher priced offerings, that are non-impulse buys, try doing webinars to sell them. Conversion rates can be much higher on these.

50. Incentivize Your Traffic To Like, Share, And Promote Your Content/Offers

If you have some great content, whether on social media or on a website or blog, consider trying to incentivize your readers to like, share, and/or promote your content or offer. You don't have to offer much. Even just mentioning that they should like or share your content for a chance to win some random prize can greatly increase your shares, visibility, traffic, and rankings! This works regardless if it's a post on social media (like Facebook), a website, or a video on YouTube.

For example, let's say that you review video games and equipment on YouTube. As a way to encourage growth, at the end of your videos, you can ask them to subscribe to your video feed, "like," and comment below for a chance to win a $50 gift card to some gaming site, a game itself, some gaming equipment, or whatever else makes sense that they'd like. You'd be shocked at the number of people who'll take advantage of this, and this can help boost your own rankings, visibility, and ability to get more traffic quite easily.

Or if you had a Facebook post or a blog post related to your gardening product, you could tell them to share and/or comment for a chance to win your gardening product for free. Even just asking people to like, comment, share, etc., (without an incentive) can greatly increase the chances of them doing it, but by incentivizing them, you'll get even more.

Takeaway: Try incentivizing your readers to like, share, comment, subscribe, etc., on your social media posts, blog posts, and videos to greatly increase the amount of traffic, additional rankings, and exposure you can get.

Conclusion

Hopefully you found at least a handful of tips that you can take fast action on. Don't feel like you have to implement them perfectly. Often times taking action fast instead of trying to perfect it will get you far better results.

And don't underestimate how even just one or two of these tips can have a drastic effect on your business. Some of these tips that we personally implemented in the past had huge effects on our businesses, despite how easy some of them were to do.

In fact, sometimes one or two of these tips can make or break a business. So, pick a few of your favorite ones and start taking action on them this week! That'll often be the difference between those who succeed and those who don't.

About the Author

Michael Rust, is a father of two girls and started his internet business career after he reached the age of 50. He has worked in various jobs after leaving school but found like many others that there were no guarantees in the world of work

He applied himself to various roles in retail, marketing and finance however it never seemed to work out in the long term due to an ever changing world.

Having gained experience in the workplace, he consequently sought other opportunities. He therefore looked for a different type of lifestyle and experimented with the world of Multi-Level Marketing for several years where he discovered his love for helping others build an extra income.

However he continued to seek further options eventually working with the great Andrew Reynolds, an £80+ millionaire with his internet marketing systems.

He has gained a great deal of information and expertise in internet marketing, online business, internet traffic generation and social Media.

Michael is now an international best-selling author, and is currently working with millionaires such as Andrew Reynolds, Tom Hua and Sean Allison to continue to build his internet businesses.

www.books-to-read.info

Further Information

We offer over 300+ e-books and e-courses and aim to provide a range of e-books and e-courses on a wide range subjects to enable you to learn further in the subjects and ideas provided in this book.

www.books-to-read.info

Michael Rust writes a regular blog for his website www.entrepreneurideas.net. Here he continues to teach and pass on his knowledge of the internet and Online business in general.

www.entrepreneurideas.net

Why don't **YOU** start your online business today?

We have everything you need.

The FUTURE Generation of Ebusiness in a Box

https://sc450.isrefer.com/go/p3/-bookstoread